For Hannah

HANNAH
IS A
BIG BABY NOW!

Helen and Clive Dorman

Paediatric Consultant:
Dr Huw R Jenkins MA MD FRCP FRCPCH

CP Publishing

Here is Hannah.

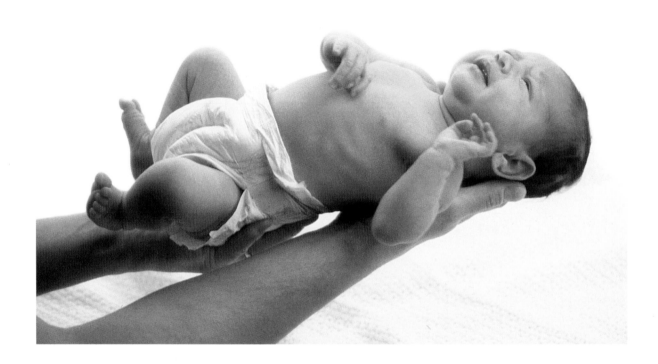

Hannah is a new baby.

She is only five days old, but she already knows her mummy's voice and smell.

She can see us and chat to us.

She needs lots of love and lots of sleep.

Do you know what you were like when you were only five days old?

Did you have any hair?

Hannah is  1 month old.

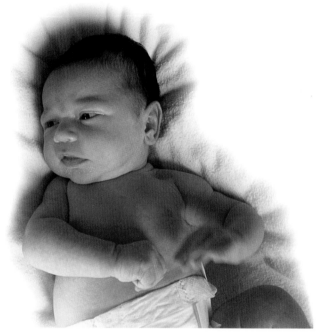

Hannah is a tiny baby but she can do lots of things for herself.

She can turn her head to follow us.

She cries to let us know she is unhappy and she smiles when she is happy.

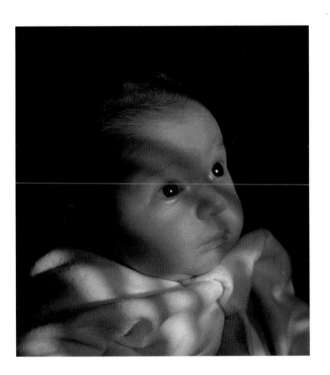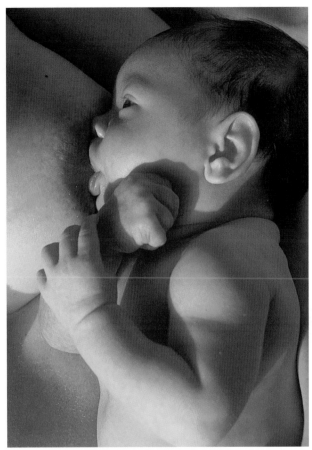

She likes to look at bright lights and have her favourite food.

What is your favourite food?

Hannah is  **2** months old.

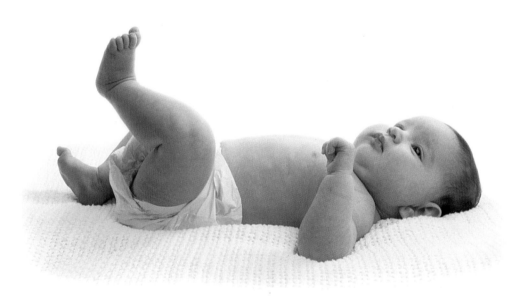

Hannah is still a tiny baby, but she is growing.
She likes to kick her legs.

She loves to look at faces and tries to copy what we are saying.

Can you pull a funny face?

Hannah is  months old.

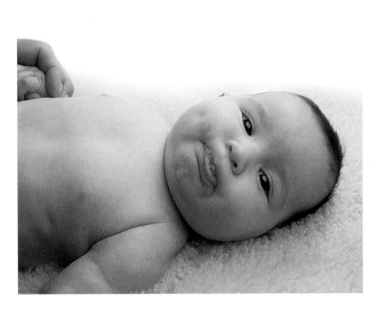 

Hannah is getting bigger.
She likes to blow bubbles and make noises!
She can put her fingers in her mouth.

She can reach out to touch her toy.

What is your favourite toy?

Hannah is  4 months old.

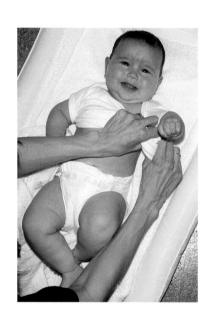 

Hannah is growing fast.

She does not like to get dressed or undressed but she loves bath time.

Do you like getting dressed? Which clothes do you like?

She tries her first food but it feels very different from the milk she is used to.

She can put her feet together.

She can take and hold a toy.

Hannah is  months old.

Hannah can nearly sit up on her own!

She can drink from her beaker and likes to bang it on the table.

She loves to play with her toes.

She discovers her reflection in the mirror.

Do you know what a reflection is?
Where else can you see a reflection?

Hannah is  months old.

Hannah can now sit up.

She can put her toe in her mouth and she can turn onto her tummy.

Can you put your big toe in your mouth?

She is cutting her first tooth and her gums are sore. She likes to suck her thumb and hold her blanket when she feels tired or sad.

Do you suck your thumb? Do you have a comforter?

Hannah is  months old.

Hannah is learning more skills as she grows.

With daddy's help she can stand up.

She likes to tip a brick out of her cup.

She can nearly crawl.

She loves to play peek-a-boo.

She now has a new tooth and chews her toothbrush.

When she is upset she reaches out to be picked up.

What colour is your toothbrush?

Hannah is  8 months old.

Hannah is getting stronger.

She can pull herself up to stand.

She has discovered new skills using her hands and teeth. She pulls hair and bites.

She likes to share her bread stick.

She tries different foods.

She can just tip up her bottle.

What is your favourite drink?

Hannah is  9 months old.

Hannah is getting more adventurous.

She always wants to climb up the stairs.

She loves to play hide and find the toy.

She can also give a toy back to you.
She finds ringing a bell very funny.

Can you count how many teeth Hannah now has?

Hannah is  10 months old.

Hannah is now very active.

She can push her walker. She can open drawers and move from one object to another.

She loves to turn the pages of her book.

She pushes food out of her mouth with her tongue to see what it looks and feels like.

She likes to blow a whistle, clap hands and play with her teddy.

Hannah is  11 months old.

Hannah has better balance and more strength.
She can crawl very fast, stand and use her trike.

Can you balance on one leg?

She loves to try and say words.

She can now hold her bottle, and she likes to spoon-feed herself.

Best of all she loves catching bubbles!

Hannah is  12 months old.

Hannah is very big. She tries to put on her socks.
She can wash her feet in the bath.
She can walk on her own!

Hannah has grown and learned a lot in her first 12 months.

Hannah *is* a big baby now!

Did you know that 12 months make up 1 year?

Do you know the names of the months of the year?

Can you point to and count the numbers?

Special thanks to Isobel McGrory, for her support, insight and inspiration.

First published in the UK in 2000 by
CP Publishing
Richmond, Surrey, UK

ISBN 1 903275 00 8

Printed in Hong Kong